Anthology Thirty-Two

Florida State Poets Association

2014

Patricia L. Stevenson, Editor

Gary Broughman, Co-Editor

Elaine Person, Co-Editor

FSPA
Publisher

ISBN: 978-0-9911189-6-0

Library of Congress Control Number: 2014953568

Printed in the United States of America

www.floridastatepoetsassociation.org

Front Cover Photos, clock-wise left to right:
Heron #16, Patricia Stevenson; *Maitland Bridge*, Elaine Person;
Gathering Seashells, Barbara Fifield; *untitled*, Niki Byram;
Bicycles at Coconut Grove, Cyndee Levy-Angulo.

Back Photo: *Ormond Beach Drive*, Elaine Person
Cover Design: Patricia Stevenson and Gary Broughman

Anthology Thirty-Two

Florida State Poets Association

2014

For forty years of FSPA poets – 1974-2014
Happy Anniversary FSPA!

To all FSPA poets over the years—past and present,
paving the way for the future.

TABLE OF CONTENTS

MEMBERS AT LARGE

FSPA 2014 POETRY CONTESTS WINNERS

2013-2014 FSPA STUDENT POETRY CONTEST WINNERS

Acknowledgements

The year 2014 brings the thirty-second year of publication of the FSPA Anthology and the fortieth anniversary of FSPA. Congratulations to Florida State Poets Association!

We extend our heartfelt thanks and appreciation to all the contributing FSPA poets for some of the best and definitely the most poems in recent years, to the poet-photographers for the many terrific photo submissions – wish we could have used all of them – and for the support and encouragement from Joseph Cavanaugh, *President of FSPA*. My personal thanks also go to B.J. Alligood, *Chair, FSPA Poetry Contests*; Janet Watson, *Chair, FSPA Student Contests*; Beth Stevenson, Diana Reynolds, Randy Krum, and to previous anthology editors J.C. Kato and Betty Ann Whitney.

Special thanks to Elaine Person and Gary Broughman for their extensive knowledge and professionalism as my co-editors working diligently with me on this edition of the FSPA anthology. You two are the best!

Patricia L. Stevenson
Chair, 2014 Anthology Editorial Board

FSPA Chapter Poets

A Gaggle of Gulls by Carol Thomas

Big Bend Poets

Tallahassee

Dixie Ann Black

Just Chasing the Sun

When I was young I ran after mother
Growing older I chased my child.
I chased after God and ran after love
But all I was doing was chasing the sun.
All I was doing was chasing the sun.

Up with the dawn to chase a dream
With its setting, still far from real
Chasing the dream which follows the earth,
Chasing the earth which follows the sun.
All I was doing was chasing the sun.

Some chase fame, some fortune and love,
Some want peace, some war, some sweet relief.
Whether war or peace, hate or love
All we are doing is chasing the sun.
All we are doing is chasing the sun.

Your schemes, my dreams, his fantasies
No more tangible, no more real.
Famine or feast, joy, sorrow or peace
We all seek that same ineffable release.
All we are doing is chasing the sun.

Ball of incandescence
Glowing brilliance, filling the skies.
Star of impermanence
Glorious splendor as it dies.
Yet all we are doing is chasing the sun.

Journey to nowhere, ego bound
Wretched and weary we seek to be found.
The rise and fall of each man's hope
Is this journey that chases the sun.
We are all just chasing the sun.

First printed in *Just Chasing the Sun,*
Dixie Ann Black, Amani Publishing, 2014

Jerry Hurley

Molly Moochers

In culinary catalogs the mushroom Morel,
freeze-dried and packaged, sterile—no smell.
A pound can be bought for hundreds of dollars
with no recollection of creeks or of hollers.

In West Virginia's hills, if you're so inclined
Molly Moochers are hidden for your eyes to find.
In shady small hollows their numbers are few,
dome-shaped sponge caps covered with dew.

My life is a river, the memories flow
and I think of adventuring long, long ago.
The creeks and hollows with deep shaded places,
Blackberries, mushrooms, Queen Anne in her laces.

Mom was excited by spring's first warm rain,
"Don't make plans for tomorrow, for they'd be in vain.
We're gonna hunt mushrooms 'til we find a mess,
after a soak in salt water I'll fry them, I guess."

We went to the woods before midday's warm sun,
beneath arches of green our searching was done.
Wet earth and damp leaves quiet under our feet,
a warm breeze was blowing—damp, musty and sweet.

They seemed to be hiding as we continued to search,
totally silent in the forested church.
We found them each nestled close to the earth
In the spot that for years had given them birth.

We carefully picked them, each a treasure indeed,
we took what we needed with no thought of greed.
I carried them home in a brown paper poke
Mom cleaned them and sliced them and put them to soak.

When ready Mom rolled them in corn freshly-milled
and fried them in butter so our noses were filled
with a smell that made it so hard to wait
for them to be ready to put on my plate.

I ate them so slowly, I savored each bite
'cause Molly Moochers are a tasty delight.
These golden fried treasures fit for a king
Are a succulent herald of what Spring may bring.

Jane Hutto

The Fourth Season

When icy winds advance your way
With whirls of frost so bold,
May you within your home be warm
Protected from their cold.

If curling drops of ice should fall
And strike you on their way,
May you withstand the frigid blast
And stand, then standing, stay.

With hope you'll wait for spring's mild breath,
Its trees of twiggy green,
When autumn's mists are far away
And winter's just a dream.

Bernita Mack

Ruminate

I stand
Amid trees
Winter snow
Blue heavens
Peaceful spot

Soft light
Calm water
Restores
Vitalizes
Helps jolt

My worn
Boring
Outlook
About life
Wakens spirit

Anomaly
No more
Will I be
Lit eyes and
Smile begin

Eileen Sperl-Hawkins

Flash of Flight

The storm rested.
Blue sky outlines the clouds.
Puddles glassed still.

Leaves cupped full.
Liquid weighed heavy
The branches' wet burden.

Like young boys school-released
The warblers shot forth
Upturning leaves.

A flash of flight
Their belly-yellow contrails
Create their own rainstorm.

Honorable mention winner, 2011 Penumbra contest,
Tallahassee Writers Association

Beth Stevenson

On Being So Near And Yet So Far

Tumultuous mixed emotions
Permeate my body, mind and soul
      Because of you—

Soul?
What is soul?

It must be that intangible which causes
      One to effervesce or wilt
It must be the depth
      the undefinable
      that gives peace, serenity

      or otherwise

Or it is the sum total of you;
      You are soul.

The tangible touching physical body
      Reacts
      Loses mind

The roving lunatic mind rages on
      And loses thought.

Patricia Lyle Stevenson

The Symphony

Sitting in my box
　At the symphony
Gilt chair beside me,
　Empty

I feel on display,
　Sitting well above the crowd below
Little black dress glittering under lights
　And rhinestones dripping
　From my ears

The musicians enter
　I check my watch
The oboist leads the tuning
　Of instruments

House lights blink　once ... twice ...
　I look behind me to
　The box curtain
　Then bend my head to the program
The house lights darken

The music rises
　I try to hear the music
It seems so far away
　And the chair beside me
　　Still empty.

Live Poets Society

Daytona Beach

Cherelyn Bush

All I Need To See

Each fall it begins sooner
Icicles and tree stands at Home Depot
In September
Christmas gift wrap at Jo-Ann Fabrics
In October
Christmas music on 100.7
In November
Black Friday at the mall
On Thursday
Greedy commercialism
Fills my eyes at any locale
Until a simple manger
Is all I need to see

Joseph Cavanaugh

New Year's Eve

The white storks are back
feasting in the rich vernal pools
near our cozy nest and winter garden

following their unique migratory pattern
feathered families guided
by the sun feed freely

we feed freely nearby
in our minds' thought patterns
create who we are

wading in our pools
in the winter sun following
our own migratory pattern

Llewellyn McKernan

Vision

Vision comes only when I'm blind.
  Then I touch each thing to see if it's mine.
  I smell the roses before they bloom.
I chew its wisdom, then swallow my food.
I hear water babies in the creek splash
  when they play, rock in their sleep.
I listen to pollen, kneaded full-grown
          to honey purling in waxen combs.

I hear music shaped just for my ears,
  enclosing the far in the very near. I follow
  the light by the warmth on my skin. To the edge
of the sunset I take it in. Twilight has footsteps
that follow me home. Night has a face I mold with
  my thumbs. Bed is a feather that teases the air.
Sleep is a silence that drifts without care
          on dreams

that move from earth to attic, from Medusa's stone
  face to Mary's—ecstatic. Though I am blind,
  still I can see how the madness of murder
turns into the sweet sun-ripened spirit,
  heady as wine. I breathe a perfume made just in
  time. I touch all the hills I used to know.
Black elephants I called them.
          Now they are snow.

Karla Linn Merrifield

Top Story: The Frond Whisperer of #E504

Boats
go by.

Sky is blue.
Cloudless.   Cool.

She listens to palm trees
tell their north-wind stories

in the high-pressure language
of the sun to a blue river

until The End arrives at midnight
under Florida's December full moon.

Alice Norman

Man Talk

it wasn't 'til after
he opened the box
took out a few pieces
put them together
kicked the box
stormed out the door
then scanned the
instructions
cursed the manufacturer
laid down on the couch

i feebly proceeded to
get it together, and failed

after he seriously studied
the manual, banging metal
said it wasn't possible
parts were missing

after he wrestled it together
it finally took shape
but it was too late to use

the grill

Miami Poets

Pinecrest

Patsy Asuncion

Children's Home

Vibrant-hot nail polish
on poetic, long fingers,
a matching red-outlined smile
lights her face.
Chanel N° 5 implicit
in her familiar garments,
Hazel must have been a beauty
in another time.

Unabashed Sara,
a toothless one-hundred-something Southern belle,
carries her baby doll and blanket
in one-shoe wonderment.
Like royalty, she walks erectly
without cane or wheelchair,
greeting anyone in the halls
like subjects in her court.

Jack, a one-hundred-four-year-old New York Jew,
sharp as a hungry merchant,
wins bingo, talks politics,
eats puréed foods, sips herbal tea.
Positive each day,
making mud pies into sweet turnovers,
never forgetting how to survive,
he is still a young immigrant.

A ninety-year-old curious toddler, Wilbur
stubbornly explores,
bouncing into unlocked cupboards,
drawers, and others' rooms.
Throwing pea soup and fighting diapers
to assert his manhood,
he bites and kicks and scratches,
to make sure he is not forgotten.

Leo, a world-war veteran
proudly wears his tattered VFW ball cap,
a badge of courage,
a reminder of youthful manhood and significance.
Hair-salon youth and manicured nails
mask his ninety-five-year-old health,
marathon smiles, and barrel-chested will—
his real badges of honor.

Without invitation,
poor memory and infirmity have moved in,
like unwelcome relatives
who stayed too long but are tolerated.
The children wander the home
searching for family and friends,
forgotten like dusty souvenirs,
replaced by events of the day.

Connie Goodman-Milone

Florida Panther Cats

Florida panther kittens rescued,
orphaned brother and sister cats
raised with great care
at conservation center.

Released back into the wilds
of the Everglades.
A cause for celebration
here in South Florida,
the preciousness of life.

First Place, South Florida Writers Association
Writing Contest, September 2013

Shirley Hill

Lorna

There is a shadow of a shadow
where her form should be.
There is a muffled echo of a faint sound
when her voice is heard.
Cats' eyes follow her.
Two dogs lick her smile from the air.
Her orchids bloom with affection while
lizards scamper about the garden
in search of her. Zoo animals
call her name in secret languages.
Rooms remember her scent.
Footsteps, light as feathers falling,
tread the stairs and walk the path
around the lake. A parade of geese
forms a processional.
Her legacy of love and kindness pulses
with each beat of our own hearts.
She is everywhere she has ever been,
yet, nowhere we can comprehend.
She is gone. She is here.

We cannot touch nor see, only
breathe her back into our lives
through memory.

Cyndee Levy-Angulo

I love that feel familiar has,

a favorite go-to piece of clothing
which lends itself to comfort, wraps
me up in an unconditional embrace

of well-being. The sense of security
and belonging I have with people
who know me in only the way time
affords long-standing friends. In those

moments of place and context, I return
to where good and almost-perfect lived
in my corner of the universe. Now,
looking through the lens of time, I know

my perspective could be colored by
the lack of well-known. Shifts in some
friendships due to unimaginable alterations,
p.j.'s that are shabby instead of cozy, the
realization I have grown in ways never
thought possible. So I make new familiar,
wonder if these memories can fill spaces
created by change and when I can, slip

into old tatty jeans and Converse, visit
with soul-friends when we find ourselves
together and be grateful for moments
I am genuinely home again.

Irvin Milowe

Seniors Dating

He had heard and disliked the Chinese proverb,
 "Shy dogs miss much meat,"
but the leftover sand in both their hourglasses
would barely cover
many remaining tides of time.

So he risked asking the lady to be his Playmate,
to even slide down his cellar door
and fill a void in his life,
knowing she was probably still too close
to her losses and old need for lady-shipping,
too uncomfortable to just have a new man in any new port,
you know, what the kids call "friends with benefits."

So he slid back down his hourglass instead,
blushing at her shot across his bow,
put away his Viagra bottle,
reminisced about an unanswered
third-grade poetry reading assignment,
about whether the "Lady or The Tiger"
would turn out to be behind the locked door.

      "STRIKE ONE!"

Elizabeth Plater-Zyberk

I Scream My Verse To The Universe

O, no, no do not touch this tomato—
pesticides!
O, no, no do not drink this water—
radioactive !
O, no, another truck is coming—
cover your face-quickly!
"Hey, no blow, no blow"
into my lungs!
Use the RAKE!
O, dear Mama Earth,
you are on the cancer floor,
pale and with balding head,
hoping to survive to
your grandchildren's joy.
I will join you soon,
but first let's RAKE the garden.

Sherwood Ross

Suicide Watch

Oh, Carolyn, my life! My love!
Yours the sin to marry me
When you loved another
To keep me in captivity
And swear 'twas love
When you only loved me
"... as a brother."
All your actions I now see
Were not designed to draw me nearer
Such as the swastika in lipstick red
You sweetly painted in my mirror.
All night I stood upon the bridge
Considering the icy river water
It was as though you ripped off an arm or leg
Had I fallen for the devil's daughter?
I was grateful for daylight and to the cop
Who asked me, "Sir, are you allright?"
And so I began again to make my way
Across the living city.
And when at last the flower vendors
Put out their flowers and their ware
I wiped my face,
And bought a rose.

Stephen Schaurer

O, Urinal

O, O, O, Miami
I should have used the men's room
before I left the restaurant
where we sipped cocktails in glasses
as big as lampshades,
and now, a few blocks up Ocean Drive
through a flow of torches and tables,
this is where I ask a drag queen
for the nearest restroom.
She tells me she's Geraldine,
Queen of South Beach,
as she takes my hand,
pulls me into the pulsating neon,
down a corridor
where she gentles me through a door—
a unisex powder room with a urinal,
thank god,
and I could just kiss her, but I don't.

Featured selection by WLRN Radio/TV,
2014 O, Miami "This is where" poetry contest

Shirley Seligman

A Special Day

On a summer day when the air sparkles,
car doors slam, front doors open,
in crowds two generations to delight the third.
Suitcases and backpacks drop.
Hugs and laughter engulf us all.
The day begins.

Young bodies run through the house,
Dry towels leaving, wet towels returning.
Reports, "he got up on skis," or "he didn't."
The day proceeds with delicious fragments
of comings and goings.
Refrigerators open and close.

Corn shucking time comes, dinner follows,
with chicken soup offered,
becoming part of their bones and memories.
Apple pie heralds the evening
Couches and floors get settled into.
Strong thumbs begin their work at video games.
The guitar comes out, singing begins.

Old folk songs and old folks' songs,
sixties Beatles' songs, sea songs,
and songs and songs
offered to the gods of
we're here together.

First published in *Second Monday Muse,*
An Anthology of South Florida Poets

Shaloma Shawmut-Lessner

I Lost The Tip Off My Finger

I lost the tip off my finger
that door was to blame
but, I better believe it
that's part of life's game.

My teacher forgot to report
the hinge was off the wall,
she had a lot of things to do
and went talking down the hall.

My teacher does this every day,
We are in the fourth grade,
boys and girls of nine and ten
we're smart and have it made

until teacher forgets to report
when walking down the hall—
and the door slips from its hinge to leave
part of my finger, bloody on the wall.

Tere Starr

My Gift

I weep for whales
beached on the shore,
for sea gulls
covered with oil,
but the only thing
I have to give is poetry.

I watch as forests
are destroyed,
as oceans are polluted
and reach inside
to find a way
to help the world survive.

The ancients knew
to honor earth,
aware of each word's power.

And now I stand
beneath the stars,
watch words
light up the sky,
then fall to earth.

 I feel her sigh.

My greatest gift is poetry.

Published in *Second Monday Muse,*
An Anthology of South Florida Poets, 2013

Barbara L. Weston

RSVP To A Former Lover

No invitation to your castle home.
No caviar or rare imported wine.
Silver and crystal can corrupt and chill
bold Bohemian bodies such as mine.
I seek instead the sultry sun,
promise of passion lighting up the sky.
Carefree caresses—Casanova's choice.
Excitement thrives and inhibitions die.
If you should tire of self-indulgent ways,
come with me and relive our yesterdays.

First Published in *Second Monday Muse,
An Anthology of South Florida Poets, 2013*

Jnita Wright

Bright Palette

I never did wear black.

I found that blood
does not show through
a simple plain red gown,
beige covers best a scar
discretion favors brown
green blends very well
around the village square
and blue will cover bruises
so the folks won't stare.

I learned to walk in monotone
to the town and back
enjoying this small triumph:

I never did wear black!

New River Poets

Pasco County

Ken Clanton

The Little Red Shoe

Sitting there beside the road
A little girl's dancing shoe.
Though damp and dirty it sparkles still
Iridescent thread of silver and red.

This symbol of her wistful dreams
In vision whirls to music's mood
Sees herself in pirouette
Does she wear a gossamer gown?

In her dreams, a woodland nymph
Or perhaps a fairy princess
Were the shoes a costume part?
I pray she just outgrew it

Are you grown and mother now
With son instead of daughter?
Or was this keepsake from your youth
Too painful to remember?

This lonely little shoe, forlorn
What story could it tell?
Was it lost or cast away?
Who are you little girl?

John F. Foster

Fine Dining

— a Petrarchan Sonnet

He entered first, three steps ahead of her,
Without a thought of holding out the door,
As if he were intending to ignore
Her token presence, knowing she'd defer.
Demanding service by the restaurateur,
He took his seat, ignoring her once more.
They sat like mannequins without rapport.
A wordless couple, disengaged they were.
Now, we may wonder why the vacant eyes,
The rote and flatly rude behavior seen,
And speculate about this loveless pair.
A dark betrayal of their nuptial ties?
Two tired souls, their lives a dull routine?
Whatever be the answer, would they care?

Second place in the *Harp Strings Poetry Journal's* Robert Frost
"Acquainted With The Night" sonnet contest.
Published in *Harp Strings,* Spring Issue, 2014

P. H. Hannaway

The Poetic Spark

Here she is,
an octogenarian poet
stretched out on a threadbare recliner.
Resting on her laurels?
Never!
She contemplates a poetic spark
just ignited in her brain.
Her right ear throbs
from a siege of shingles
and her slender shoulders ache,
but she reaches for paper and pen
to capture the essence of her verse.
From outside comes
the insistent crow of a pet rooster.
The mood is broken.
She rises with difficulty,
answering his plaintive call.
It's food he needs,
Not Poetry! She sighs.
Another unproductive day.

Beverly A. Joyce

Sweet Dreams In Fields Of Green

A very nice way
To pass a lazy day,
In sleep that's serene,
Sweet dreams in fields of green.

Just to lie upon the grass
And let the idle time pass,
Envisioning sights yet to be seen,
Sweet dreams in fields of green.

Close your eyes and doze,
Drift into peaceful repose,
Break from the old routine,
Sweet dreams in fields of green.

Janet Watson

To Know Flight

So often I have watched doves rise,
Into the dawn or twilight skies
And guessed the gladness wings must be,
But I can only fantasize.

I gaze upon each soaring bird
Where silky milk-white clouds are stirred.
A hawk, it was, who sent a call.
That free and joyful cry, I heard.

His call invites, but earthbound-I
Can only stare into that sky
And wonder how my life would be
If I had wings, and I could fly

And dip through trees as cardinals do,
Or flock with herons, gliding through
A wetland green, or climb quite high
With gulls above the sea-waves blue.

I wonder, too, why fragile things
Like bees and butterflies have wings,
As do most gnats and other bugs.
Do I annoy with wonderings?

Not one winged creature makes demands.
Such innocence God understands.
They simply are. They soar and fly
And never wish for human hands.

First place, 2013 FSPA LaVaughn Hess Award

Betty Ann Whitney

After The Settling Of White Noise

At dinner today, I scanned the newspaper
A half-inch headline caught my eye:

You'll never be any younger than you are today.

Eyes bright with that fabulous notion,
head filled with certain choices of thought,

suddenly then, I'm driving back
to buy me those bright red jeans.

Orlando Area Poets
Maitland

Sonia Jean Craig

Portrait Of A Woman

The soft white glitter
On her eyelashes
Greets the saffron light of the morning

Red lips drink in
The amusing passage
Of her magazine

Fuchsia flowers grace
Indigo black hair
Like an antennae of petals
Dancing with her mind.

Alice Friedman

Teddie's Ashes

Teddie's ashes were divided in half
or so we thought
Teddie was split in two equal parts
more or less
Teddie's ashes in two equal parts, more or less,
were put on the floor of my car and
half of Teddie was scattered in the Gulf
half of Teddie was scattered in North Carolina
but some of Teddie remained in that car
and I traded it in.

Part of Teddie floats free in the warm salty Gulf
part of Teddie flies wild in the mountain wind
and part of Teddie is stuck in that car
boogieing down the road perhaps
basso booming acid rock mocking his critic's ear
and Teddie won't have it.
How do you spoze he handles that?

Honorable Mention, Chronicle 2001
Dr. Stephen Caldwell Wright Poetry Awards
Published in *What Now, Courage? A collection of poems*
by Alice R. Friedman

Janay Garrick

Bridalveil Fall
Yosemite, California

I open Wendell Berry,
turn pages which dispense
the smoke of firewood
and clean air, the clouds
and crisp of paper sack sleeping
bags have captured
and bottled the scent that's come to be you.

I pray for the peak of eighty-eight-million-year-old
mountains to redeem
what you packed and took to Arizona.

Wendell looks at trees and hears
a primal Sabbath hymn.

I need such a hymn
to live and die inside this skin
stretched like a pomegranate broken
open, my heart buried in a small patch
work of earth, I pick up rocks

      pile
      them
      one
      by
      one

like an altar
next to an impossible
crossing of river
without fallen tree

   rope
   or friend
   to tether me.

I sit inside the navy blue shadow
of a granite wall, the cold of ancient
estuaries and glacial roots
springing up inside of me.

I trail behind the others
crossing soft snow meadows
so I can cry, God's majesty
eclipsing my sorrow.

Now I've come to the roar
of Bridalveil Fall
and the question I must leave there—

Catherine Giordano

A Kaleidoscope Of Words

Words rattle around in my brain
Like the bits of colored glass inside a kaleidoscope.

Shake them up
And they form beautiful patterns.

Shake them again
And they reform,

    A totally different pattern
    As beautiful as the one before.

With each shake a pattern is lost.
The words demand that I write them down.

The instinct for self-preservation.

Previously published in *The Poetry Connection*
by Catherine Giordano, 2011

Russ Golata

That Certain Midnight

Always think of the beginning
A fresh start with a new look
Looking ahead, never behind

For a moment you turn ...
The struggles of everyday
Drown in a sea of acid rain

There is no poetry here
The bad guys are gaining
The wolves of Wall Street feeding

It's twelve o'clock around the world
Hold your head up now
Look tomorrow straight in the eye

Use the strength of the sunrise
Feel the pull of duty of the moon
The first day of the new beginning

Everything looks so fresh and clean
You take the first steps into the future
A new year, a new day ... begins

Sierra Goodrum

Museum Of Spring-Time

He wrote, "Sierra you are a museum of
Spring-time." These words have been growing
Inside me since February of this year. I've waited
And waited for them to tarnish or fade, but they
Have not. They are true. In the instant
he met me—a hero of my own; wordsmith of
colossal size, a genuine heart and a steady pen
to change others with—*I was written.* Summed
up in eight words. With a signature at the end.
I couldn't breathe, *how did he know?*

How did he know I was a whitewashed home,
Cracking, where my strength that preserved
Rose up to share its green beauty? How did he
Know my resilience? That I was a home for many,
A place of rest for a few and a safe house?

Yes, I am a museum of spring-time, holding all
The good seeds till winter fades. I hold
Precious things closer and closer—to warm them,
Encourage their growth, call them out to take root.

"It may be cold now, but the sun—it will come."
Of all the shaken winters I've become fond of, it
Was the first time I heard I wasn't what I had accepted.
I wasn't the barren cold, bitter or unwanted. I didn't chase
others away with my howl of warning. I wasn't the ice
that made others slip. I wouldn't be the beauty that
turned into a dark and muddy version of myself. I wasn't
the cold that encompassed holidays, and I wasn't
the wind that kisses your cheeks with an envy at
your warmth. No, I am a promise. I am life, I am light,
I am what makes people shed their skins of
Layers and call them out to join. I was what came
After the break. I am the one who grows with you
Till the end. The sweet fruit of hard work. The taste
Of joy. I am love. I am all these things.

I do not resent winter, I admire its wild nature.
But I am no longer bound by the cold center, I am
Growing with a fresh start. With a clear mind of,
"I am what comes after death, a new life."

I am a museum of spring-time.

Peter M Gordon

Three Points

Feet, one inch behind the line
I stand alone, knees bent
Hear the sharp thump of ball
On polished wooden floor

A white and black shape streaks
Down the center of the lane
Twin towers in blue
Leap with arms upraised
At their apogee my point guard
Hurls the orange sphere to me in the corner

The ball thuds into my hands
I push it to the middle of my chest
Move my right hand
Just below its center
Eyes fixed just behind the red rim
My arms form interlocking angles
Above my eyes
My knees start bending and I

Inhale.
Sound ceases.
No sneaker squeaks
Or trash talk
The rim twenty-two feet away
Ten feet up
Looks as close as a trash can
Under my desk

I levitate
Flick my right wrist
The sphere kisses
My fingertips
Arcing toward ceiling
Then falling
Through the rim
With a small shiver of net

I'm already running back
As if I could pass this miracle
Any time I want

Monica Harper

Trayvon

Not guilty, not guilty
is all I heard in my ears
As my heart started to pound
and my eyes filled with tears.

There is no *I* in the word *team,*
but what does that really mean?
If we subtract *us* from the word *justice,*
it becomes pretty lean.

Matter of fact, it wouldn't make sense,
Like being killed
under a false pretense.
I want to rid the world of these dudes
called Racism, and Sexism
And replace them with Compassion and Social Activism.

I guess what I am trying to say is Race,
Class, and Gender will not pull us apart
But will it keep another seventeen-year-old
hooded-sweatshirt-wearing kid
from safely making it home in the dark?

He never made it to his father's home
and now there is a member missing
from the class of 2014.
A member never to be heard
and never to be seen!

No senior pictures,
No Grad Bash
No reason to send out graduation invitations,
or college applications

Just the memory of a terrible night gone wrong
And the commitment of a people to rise and overcome!

Carlton Johnson

Taking A Leap
On July 18, 1955

Weldon Kees walked
                    the span

and found the only way
                    up and out

from being   down and out

was taking   a leap

a leap of faith–
                    lessness

limbs and torso   flailing at the thin air

before finding home

                    in the hard pristine waters

beneath the twin towers

of the Golden Gate

an empty VW

keys in ignition, radio playing

static like gravel on the ocean floor

Estelle Lipp

The Pen Leads The Way

Playing with words, refining thoughts
the pen navigates the way.
Carving a path through the mumble jumble,
avoiding the chaos of all other sounds
competing for attention, pulling me away.

I hold onto the pen like a life jacket,
without which I would drown
in a sea of noise,
unable to hear my heartsounds.

Ngan Ling Lung

Departure

I left
You wept
You are alone in my absence
I grieve and long for your presence

I left so that you may grow
You wept so that I may know
Love is greater than separation
Return: I see you a new creation

Holly Mandelkern

The Eye Of The Storm

Out of the whirlwind
Van Gogh's starry night
turns to storm—
roaring waves of wind
swirl around its eye,
detaching details from the firmament,
spitting oceans as it spins,
staring down the light.
The eye brews chaos in the white
spaces where all attachments cease:
humans scatter into dry nests,
birds hide in tottery houses,
trees twist toward terra firma.
From this drenched land, life forms
long for the eye to wink us back
to Vincent's night
of just wind
and luster of light.

Frank T Masi

My Werewolf

My werewolf lurks inside—
a beast caged by life's demands.
It's perched behind owl eyes,
in my breast and in my hands.

By day I walk upright
proud to be my own man.
Each evening I pray when I awake,
No blood will stain my hands.

But sometimes at the strangest hour
My hate grows strong, and I feel the power.

I seek to kill, if I can't I maim
I stalk the weak and attack the lame.
I kill to survive, and survive to kill.
I'm damned by the holy and blessed by the evil.

No one can exorcise this dark curse.
Churches and schools just make it worse.
Addicted to blood, appeased by death's grace,
I revel in squalor and thrill in disgrace.

As daylight approaches, I'm breathless and weak,
I curse my own hate and turn it on me.
The werewolf recedes to his private lair,
and the man returns to the body he shares.

And then it appears—a face in the door,
a heaven-sent love that makes my heart soar.
As I reach for her hand, I swear evermore,
the werewolf is dead, and I pray it's for sure.

Elaine "Lainie" Person

Without A Man   The Joy of Now

She travels 'round the world.
She does everything she can,
but she feels her world is empty
since she doesn't have a man.

She's been to Greece,
Madrid, and Nice
and fished in Ketchikan.
It all was great,
but she does hate
her life without a man.

She went to Venice,
Wimbledon for tennis,
and traveled Pakistan,
walked Blenheim Palace
till she had a callus,
but did not find a man.

She saw ruins in Rome
and froze in Nome
and was Bruce Springsteen's fan
at the Jersey Shore,
but she wants more.
She wants to find a man.

She "did" L.A.,
sailed Chesapeake Bay,
and swam in the Yucatan.
She danced to disco
in San Francisco
all without a man.

She travels with pride
far and wide,
even saw Afghanistan.
She has good friends,
but her joy depends
on if she has a man.

Her trips are great
she just can't wait
to see Jamaica, man.
She keeps so busy
it makes her dizzy
searching for a man.

She loves Bombay,
travels all the way
For a concert to the Isle of Man.
Yet her heart is heavy
as a '64 Chevy
when driving without a man.

Caught up in the search for tomorrow,
she misses the joy of now.
She must learn she can be whole
without a wedding vow.

"Country Joe" Rosier

Writing A Poem

I sit and read
a poem I've written
one that came out
of the blue

Now I try to create
a new poem
one that is original
and true

Yes, it is hard for me to start
and write a poem
when it doesn't
come from the heart

But, there are times
I get the urge
the juices flow so fast
I come out with a word
Then another
they tumble out
so quickly

The thought
the inspiration
the "aha"
of it all

But, now I sit
and try to write
when the juices just won't flow
I tell myself
and I should know
be patient and just wait

soon they will erupt
in a torrent
of words
so fast
I can't
write
them
all.

Poetry for the Love of It
Tallahassee

Charles Hazelip

An Arlington Statue

In Arlington Cemetery heroes are many,
Their headstones often adorned with wreaths
Of battle monuments there are plenty,
But only one statue found able to breathe.

Daily the statue takes her position,
Solitary, bereft, a heart-broken soul.
For her wreaths are never necessary,
Nor is shelter from rain, snow, heat, or cold.

Sorrowing, grieving, the loving statue
Sits all day by the grave of her son.
He is back from Iraq draped in a flag,
Dead, making war for Washington.

Every day she is there, an icon of tragedy
Among battle monuments adorned with wreaths.
In Arlington Cemetery heroes are many
But, only one statue barely able to breathe.

Third Dimension Poets of Broward

Broward County

Andrea Calia

Take My Hand

Walk through the meadow with me
  Mama, take my hand
Let's explore our surroundings
I want to roll around in the grass
Letting the sun shine in my eyes
Look at the different shapes the clouds form
  Mama, take my hand
I want to run try to catch butterflies
Listen to the birds chirping
Oh look at all the dandelions
Let's pick one, close our eyes, make a wish
My wish is my mother was really here with me
So I could say to her
  Mama, take my hand

Jody Fallabel

At the meadow's edge
Deer retreat behind branches
Their dark eyes peering

Kerrin Farr

Escaped Thoughts

I can no longer pay attention
Her voice so boring
Stepping away my thoughts drift
Looking out the window
I see vibrant gleaming leaves
Dancing butterflies, freedom celebrated
Freedom from which I do not have
And Yearn for.

Lita Moffa

Yesterday

That time you captured me with pensive eyes,
I think I fell in love with you that day.
This came to both of us as a surprise.

Crowds gathering below a cloudless sky.
Those people on the path began to fade.
That time you captured me with pensive eyes.

I left the sculpture garden on the rise.
Ran quickly past the children on parade.
This came to both of us as a surprise.

I thought you called my name above the cries
But that could be a fantasy I made.
That time you captured me with pensive eyes.

To hold onto this moment we both tried.
Time fell between us and your feelings strayed.
This came to both of us as a surprise.

Sweet evenings that dissolved in carnal sighs,
are lost because of your chance to betray
That time you captured me with pensive eyes.
This came to both of us as a surprise.

Louis Robert Moffa

Day's End

Sun races to edge the horizon, coloring
summer's sky the rich copper hue of
Vin Santo.
My mouth is parched.
Hungry for taste of the grape.
Fingers embrace icy moisture
of a carafe, tipping sunlit liquid
Into a fragile glass.
Intoxicating scent.
A perfect vintage kisses my mouth.
Recalling lazy days in vineyards of
Barberino Val D'Elsa,
I soar to the sky

I view.

Christine Jacobson-Ralston

Dark rain clouds forming
Cool gusty winds approaching
Swallows flying south

Regina Skane

Pretending

Hats, gloves, long dresses, beads.
The Magic Box!
What character would I be?

Ginger Rogers with swirling skirt?
Or Della Street with suit and purse?

Rich and famous, definitely,
Pretending in my fantasy.

Each day would excitement bring
And gather 'round me sweet success
As I envisioned happiness.

The Magic Box has now become
Walls of life with costumes hung
From every phase and hoped for dream,
And all is never what it seems.

The only "dress up" worn again
Is the mask I wear

   To pretend.

Tomoka Poets

Ormond Beach

B.J. Alligood

Elephant Ears

Strong veined and curly edged
a proud testament to their
African four-footed namesake
as they riffle in the breeze and
stoically sustain the boiling oxygen.

Florida humidity keeping them from
drooping in the oppressive heat
as we bipeds drag our feet
and pant open-mouthed
between sagging tendrils of hair.

Cracks of lightning herald the
descent of liquid boulders.
Heaven's offer thundering
like a herd of zebra
leaving bright clear crystals
scattered among the waterproofed
green canvas of their hills and valleys.

Freddie (Travallion) Booth

Awash In A Sea Of Poetry

Awash in a sea of poetry without a Webster's life vest
Floundering amongst letters and sparkling words of
emotional images illuminated by daylight.
Pictures painted abundantly and
excruciatingly vivid by others.
The level of education is in the clouds above.
The tide pushing me ashore where
my poems lay like broken seashells on the beach,
waiting for my memory to recall the essence of
thoughts long ago forgotten
to put them back together again.
Trying to stay afloat in waves of anonymity
where accolades would buoy me up.
Where derision would let me drown and yet
my muse holds me up
haltingly.
My feet touch something glimmering below.
A morsel of something retrieved from the deep ...
Then returned to shore far, far away on the horizon.

Walter "Teal" Mims

As Far As The Eye Can See

The landscape of the Florida marshy
Hammock teems with serenity.
It abounds with the harmony of life
Having been invaded with the souls of
Nature's imperfect quiddity.
Evolution is but an affair between flora and fauna
Demanding propagation and randomness.
The rains rain and the rivers flow.
Returning their life's blood to the beginning.
Having been consummated
It begins yet again—differently.

G. Kyra von Brokoph

Desires Dark Brother

A murmur—mocking as you go,

A shrug, a glance, an untuned smile.

Growling engine, tires grinding,

Crawling slow

Squirming a reluctant mile.

I wade the shallow waters

Of the surf that

Cool the burn of your lips.

Making love that afternoon

Would have seemed as natural as

The rhythm of the rolling waves.

Was desire's dark brother,

Fear,

Watching over us so dim?

Lest we drive the bearing wave and surge?

Yours of the undertow of my allure.

Mine of the injurious cresting saboteur

Ebbing a tempestuous merge.

Will you help me banish him?

Until then, mock not

My *wonderful way with words*:

Desire's camouflaged caress,

Soft touch screen decoys fluoresce

And coruscate unfurling

Splays of shimmering bait.

Until then the wounded

Dusk and dawn,

The wanton wake and sleep.

Along the haunted, wailing surf

I wade the waters dark—

And weep.

Gary Broughman

A Rare Flower

A rare flower in a quiet corner
of the meadow steals the gaze
of the few souls who happen by,
surprising curious eyes with blossoms
blending petals so dark and so fair,
an unmatched summer snowflake,
perfectly itself in all of nature.

Some unfold as if made of light,
fragile as fine Alabaster, delicate
as the mouth of a finely thrown vessel,
and yet inviting in all things,
gathering, restoring all things,
living the eternal assurance
of mother sun.

And within this peerless flower,
lush petals deep and dark arise,
standing side by side
with translucent sisters—
a vision to surprise heart
and mind, as if an artistic God
deigned to teach the world's eyes
the art of contrast, fear and beauty
woven together in paradox, a veil
pulled back on the hope born
in the first moment of creation—
oneness out of diversity
in each and among all,
revealing in living form
the pattern of God's intentions
for a universe made from love.

Niki Byram

Widow To The Blue Glow

Much to my chagrin,
You left me for the one
With the black Bakelite complexion.
You know, the one with
The big face measured on the diagonal;
The one with the permanent blue glow.

Every night you reach out to her,
And she always comes on for you.
Catering to your every whim,
She's taught you just about
Everything you'd ever need to know,
Under the tutelage of
The blue glow.

She never asks you any questions,
Or ever interrupts your show.
With the flick of your wrist,
And as quickly as you can point the remote,
Voilà! It's done.
Your wish is her every command.
On you she does surely dote,
While sitting in the corner on her stand.

Bleary-eyed and blurry-brained
You became enamored as
Your affection for her continued to grow,
Your face reflecting fascination,
As it became bathed in the blue glow.

Slack-jawed, face filled with stupor,
I'd seen this look of rapture before.
Imagine my distress at your
Infatuation with your late night mistress.
I watched in horror as
I became a widow to the blue glow.

Mitzi Coats

Grandfathered

Thick in bark and leaf
bent and knotted as befits its height and berth
shelter to squirrels and nesting birds
to mama raccoon with baby wedged
in its sturdy limbs
survivor of storms, woodpeckers, and drought,
the old oak's lofty canopy shades
our company house built in 1951
and the remnants of past lives that linger still:
a tree house dangles by rusty nails
a steppingstone cradles the footprint of a child

and sometimes, before sleep comes,
I think I hear the muffled tones
of television and squeaking recliner
in the living room,
as the widowed owner of this house
through forty years of marriage before us
rocks away loneliness
   —ah, it's probably just the railroad tracks
humming with freight
or wind shaking branches against the roof

and yet, last spring I saw my neighbor,
who lived her last three years in a nursing home,
in ethereal fleshiness surveying boundaries
before she faded into air behind the oak.
Like her, with one foot
still in this world and one in the next,
the roots of the oak staked two-hundred years ago
now straddle yard and road
directly in the path of a planned sewer line.

Barbara Fifield

Chewing Gum Together

As I pop gum in my mouth

I think of you, Enid, chewing gum.

You liked it, too,

Especially Wrigley's Spearmint Gum.

I prefer Chiclets—

But a stick of gum will do.

I bought you a double pack of Wrigley's

while you were in rehab.

You thanked me, afterward.

Cracking gum gave you pleasure, you said,

While waiting for friends to visit.

Now you lie in Indiana in a grave

I'll never travel to

But down here, I'll visit you in my mind

and remember how we chewed gum, together.

Colleen O'Leary

Home At Last

As distance closes in over yonder hill
Not knowing why it's beckoning against thy will

Only sound of strong wind blowing
Raging waves crashing against the shore

Why this beckoning?
Why me?
What is this mystery that is upon thee?

My heart beats stronger with fear
With each step getting nearer

The sun rises and warms my soul
Fear for nothing more
Towering high upon this hill

A calming peace comes upon thee
It's waiting Angels that I see

As I begin to pray
I feel the presence of my loved ones
To help guide me along the way

All that pain is in the past
For I am home

Home at Last

Carol Thomas

Old Woman Poet

tells truth slant, the way she came to know it;
she will tell you we began hermaphroditic, unified,

comingled self in other, the way a mother carries
deep within new life repeating all that we have been;

then sometime in evolution's history, a radical,
a seismic split, two human species out of one;

she finds no other explanation of extremes:
the warrior ones, the birthing ones,
the old and helpless ones;

she'll explain seed time, chemicals, quarks,
particles, and war; she will tell you how to go to death

unbittered and relinquished; she will tell you every
woman's heart holds mercy, grief, and love,

anodynes against our dread; forked creatures unaccommodated
but by love shaman,
she will tell you how to hold each other

how to keep the small ones warm throughout a winter night
show them how to find the milky way, stars, aurora borealis

home

Joe Perrone

Falling Rainbows

Glistening, glimmering shards of light;
Reflective, shimmering, cold and bright.
Each twirling, swirling, spinning around
Floating rapidly down toward the ground.

Crystals bursting like snowflakes in flight,
Reflective, sparkling, a one-time sight;
Each one a prism disbursing light,
Each a rainbow, refracting sunlight.

Each crystal a colorful shard of glass,
Exploding outward as if en masse;
Forming together halos of light
Framing within a horrible sight.

Halos encasing darkness within;
Surreal beauty surrounding the din.
Rainbows of colors harboring death,
Catching our eye while we held our breath.

Halos of colors framing the dead;
A glimmering sight so full of dread.
Reflective colors for all to see;
A beauty surreal that should not be.

A crystal display affecting all,
Holding eyes transfixed, watching it fall;
Giving to all a colorful sight.
No photo that day captured it right.

Those who stayed to watch, saw as it fell,
A beauty and darkness brought from hell;
A sight no one thought could ever be
'Til the day that changed our history.

A day so clear with no morning haze;
One of those "good to be alive" days
With much light for a crystal display
For all to witness that fateful day.

A once in a lifetime light display
Bringing darkness on a sun-filled day;
A sight seen but once, so they did tell,
That is, 'til the second tower fell.

Mary-Ann Westbrook

Twilight On The Beach

white caps curl
over the outer
sandbar spraying
spume into fading
sunlight
its energy spent
the sea slides
softly over bare
feet
ghost crabs and
long legged birds
scatter in
receding tide
like strewn seeds
searching
for existence

Members At Large

Palm at Sunset by Cyndee Levy-Angulo

Mary Jo Balistreri

The Bookmobile

Every two weeks, we'd search the horizon
for a distant cloud of dust. It never failed us.

Into the dry dirt lot the bookmobile rolled toward
a long line of small bodies baking in South Dakota heat.

Finally, finally when the door to the trailer opened,
the bookmobile lady in wire-rimmed glasses appeared,

her face a text of perception. Black hair swept high on her head,
she stood in her crisp white blouse.

One by one she handed us a towel to wipe sweaty hands
before allowing us to cross her threshold.

Inside, a fan blew cool air, and we felt it a holy place
so different from our homes.

I thumbed through pages of Scarlet O'Hara,
but Nancy Drew proved
more exciting in her blue roadster as did the flying flanks
of *The Black Stallion* and Flame, manes streaming free.

But it was Francie who changed my life.

Like the tree of heaven that sprouted between cracked cement
outside her Brooklyn tenement,

she encouraged me to push ever upward, to rise from my own
dirt lot,
and to grow,
grow green and alive.

Published on *Your Daily Poem,* 2013

Pat Bastendorf

Leaf Raking

What fun raking leaves,
bonding in the brisk breeze,
he with his toy rake, helping.
I feign anger when
he spreads leaves again
by jumping and rolling and yelping.

We start burning piles.
The smell goes for miles
and can't be described, just remembered.
I often think back
to the leaf-fire's crack
when city with nature was tempered.

Years later that tree
still holds memories for me
when he visits with grandson and mower.
His son has to stay
in, out of the way
while he breaks tradition with blower.

When they drive home
with thoughts of their own,
our heir in the back uninspired,
I can't help but wonder
what memories he'll ponder
when he sits alone and retired.

First printed in chapbook, *Leaf Raking and Other Poems*,
Pat Bastendorf, 2004

Gail Denham

Rock Face

Two million years, I been stuck here,
winter, lightning, rain. Oh I really
hate rain. It's like eating ice cream
with a cracked tooth.

Then there is the badger. Mean, spiteful
monster. Moved right into the vacant
area at my feet. Never asked, never
even says, "Howdy," as he blithers about.

It's come to me that I could be settled here
for eternity, smaller with erosion as my sand
particles drop off, granduncle to scores
of badger litters, forming new splits each year.

Guess I'd like a change. If a nice big flood
should come along and loosen my footing.
I could tumble to the edge of everything,
see how they treat their rocks over there.

From *On the Way to Everywhere*,
a chapbook by Gail Denham, 2009

R. Patrick Elliott

Perfidious Eros

Love comes to call in many ways,
> But very rarely ever stays.
Love that's shallow, love that's deep;
> Love is seldom ours to keep.

Hearts are given, taken, shattered;
> Tender hearts are wounded, battered.
Tender hearts will harden fast,
> For tender hearts so rarely last.

Judith Krum

One Voice, Then Two

The fanfare in the skies tells us they're here.
The beating wings keep rhythm with the heart.
The geese are flying north again this year.

Cast in their V, they suddenly appear.
We stop, look up, unable to depart.
The fanfare in the skies tells us they're here.

One voice, then two, then scores dispel the drear
From souls too long without their grace and art.
The geese are flying north again this year.

Their bodies glide, with necks thrust out, austere.
In them we see what air and sun impart.
The fanfare in the skies tells us they're here.

The trumpets and the flourish of our sphere,
The call, the swell of wings, our counterpart.
The geese are flying north again this year.

Their need is flight, the freedom but to steer
Their lives each spring along time's unknown chart.
The fanfare in the skies tells us they're here.
The geese are flying north again this year.

Originally published as "Villanelle" in
The Berkshire Review, Vol. 7, Spring, 1999, Lenox, MA

Charles Larsen

Homecoming

Seeing military greeted thus, I sigh
family and friends, dignitaries hail
it sometimes brings tears to my eye

Recall how rapidly the time does fly
from time of riding across the rails
military being greeted thus, I sigh

Don't get me wrong, I do know why,
earned their greetings, and the hails
it sometimes brings tears to my eye

Arrived one day, my head held high
from sea off Korea, we did not fail
seeing military greeted thus, I sigh

Off the train, duffle bag held high
campaign ribbons, so far did we sail
it sometimes brings tears to my eye

No father, mother, no one nigh,
rode streetcars, waited on steps
seeing military greeted thus, I sigh
it sometimes brings tears to my eye

Trudy Livingstone

Martha

A
Beautiful butterfly
Danced through my life
A brief pause
In the motion of eternity
An elegant beauty
Eyes afire
With love of life
And depth of soul
She alighted in my life
Smiled, connected
And moved on ...

Scott Mayo

That We May Bear True Witness

Summertime, and the living is dying
Climate change, digital age, overpopulation rage
The best of times and the worst of times before
Only the worst of times now
Sky really is falling
End really is near
Not of the planet
Just the world
End of family
End of community
End of our country
End of humanity
Still God sees the truth, but waits
What purpose do truthful writers have
When truthful writing is no longer valued
Why does not God deliver us
From this historical hell
Perhaps that we may bear true witness
To this end
That we may chronicle it, record it
On paper
That when the last artificial light goes out
Something will remain
In writing
To tell what happened here.

Ruth Nott

Voyager

Adrift on a sea of memories
Alone with the wind and the waves.
The painful take flight on the wings of gulls;
Wrapped in sunlight, the best are saved.
Rocked like a babe in the womb
I succumb to the sway of the sea,
Asleep in visions of yesterday
As each wave brings you back to me.

Adrift on a sea of memories
Awaiting the coming storm
When the gulls will take refuge beside me
And the pain that they carry transform
My sunlight to darkness and turmoil
As lightning streaks turbulent skies
Illuminating my guilt and my shame
And the fear lurking deep in my eyes.

Adrift on a sea of memories
Alone as the storm subsides,
Hearing their cries as the gulls depart,
I awake drifting home on the tide.
Reality shakes the awakening
As dream ships and waves disappear.
Today takes shape in the morning mist,
A new voyage surprisingly near.

Dan Pels

Eclipse

Alone,
camping in
the moonlight,
I fire my rifle
at nearby trees
but I miss.
Since there are
no barns, I
shoot at the moon—
missed twice, but
on the third shot,
I hit the man
right between the eyes.
He blinks
fuming with anger.
Now, everything is totally dark.
I'm still
at a loss for words.

Elda Nichols

New Adult

I'm eighteen, and
Free as a bird
I'll do what I please,
Parents can't say a word
There's no more telling me
What I can do
I'm an adult,
And between me and you
I'm spreading my wings,
Soon to take flight
I'll be giving my folks
Tense, sleepless nights
I'll smoke and I'll drink
And have lots of fun
Forgetting my past,
I'll stay on the run
My parents are oddballs,
Not very hip
I'll try every way to
Give them the slip
There's no way I care
What I'll put them through
It feels good to hurt them—
Make them feel blue
Their love and devotion
I've had all my life

I'm eighteen, so what if
I'm bringing them strife
I've had the best schools,
Clothes and a home
Forget all that stuff,
Now, it's just text and phone
My new friends are crude,
But don't criticize
We do tattoos and piercings
And tell lots of lies
Maybe someday
I'll come to my senses
But till that day comes,
I'm burning my bridges!

Jeani Picklesimer

Oasis Of My Pen

As tender blades of grass begin to sway
And dance to whispers of the summer wind,
I think of us, our love, and yesterday.
Though you are gone, my heart and I pretend
That we can hear you in the autumn eve,
When patchwork leaves bow low to kiss the ground.

When angels came, you had to take your leave,
And rest awhile, where silence is the sound,
O, Heart! You make oasis of my pen
That drowns the wretched dryness on this page,
Propelling me to lovely days of when
This empty songster left the gilded cage
And fled to places where I touched perfume!
And there I sought and found a soft embrace.
I hugged a tender bud and watched it bloom,
Until the snowflakes froze upon its face.
Because my shattered heart had stopped its breath,
It did not seem to try to understand
That on the day you closed your eyes in death,
You left the spirit of your guiding hand.

And now 'tis time for magic of the spring,
When things set out to stir and be reborn!
My soul begins to quiver and to sing!
You stroked my rusty pen this April morn!
O, Heart! You make oasis of my pen,
To fill the emptiness that chases me.
So, I will dream, until we meet again.
Our souls shall then find rhyme eternally!

First Place, KSPS Contest 2009;
Second Place, Masters Award, *The Poet's Pen*, Winter 2012

Dennis Rhodes

Sunrise For Emily

The sun slipped in my window
To see if all was well.
He'd come a frightful distance—
As far as I could tell!

A dream rushed off unfinished,
Its plot in disarray,
Powerless to hold my whim
In light of a new day.

I sat upon a pillow,
The sun preferred to stand,
Yet another suitor
Begging for my hand.

He filled my room with wonder.
His presence overpowered.
Lesser mortals than myself
Would have quaked and cowered.

"About my proposition—"
He cut right to the chase,
"May I spend a lifetime
Shining in your face?"

I laughed, then shut the window
Feeling quite supreme
And in the blessed darkness
Went to chase a dream.

Mary Rogers-Grantham

Come On, Now

Where I come from
poetry grows wild along highways.
Words marinate in shopping malls,
and titles emerge on Pharaonic days.

Where I come from
blues breed Hallelujahs.
Hosannas nest in the wind,
and prayers are poetry at work.

Where I come from
pantoums narrate events,
headlines become found poems,
and haiku gives birth to nature.

Published in *Under A Daylight Moon*
by Mary Rogers-Grantham

Evelyn Ann Romano

Morning

Awake,
I find evil at the door.
Bundled tight in a box
smiling white, wide grins
squeezing me back into dreams:
kaleidoscopic, zombie-like
clouds weaving through days, years
of clotted life. Replaying loss, fear,
frustration, all holding hands. Do they
mean what they say, these taunting,
teasing flares of insight? Should I
clear them from my plate,
file as useless,
or pay attention?
The day outside is the same—
sun sneaking up,
moist warming air
singing in the distance.

First place winner, Tampa Writers Alliance 2011 Annual Contest
Published in *Wordsmith 2011— Tampa Writers Alliance Literary Journal*

FSPA 2014
Poetry Contests
First Place Winners

Trio of Pipers by Patricia Stevenson

Category 1: FSPA Free Verse Award

Mary Jo Balistreri
Genesee Depot, WI

Speaking In Tongues

> *"When one tugs at a single thing in nature, he finds*
> *It attached to the rest of the world."* —*John Muir*

Before the spoken word—the rush and roar of a waterfall
down walls of Vishnu schist,
the more muffled pitch that tumbles
among jumbled talus slopes, the unidentified
melodies of birds
that ricochet off looming basalt, cascade
down slick-rock cliff,
rise and fall in a crevice—original bass of stone, earth key
of multifarious voices intertwining and overlapping.
Like music, speech of another kind:
lightning cracking and singing the air, an eagle's scree
plummeting toward prey, shuddering and stopping time;
a heron's hoarse shriek disappearing
into a soundless blue blur;
the more subtle dry-boned rustling
of sage, howling and sighing
of wind, the vibrating dark. Dialogue of silence and sound,
ebb and neap, systole and diastole,
rhythms that enjoin or scatter our paths,
the thread we contour our lives around, labyrinth
that returns us to the place where we spoke our first word.

Category 2: FSPA Formal Verse Award

Joyce Shiver
Crystal River, FL

Technicolor Evening

I'm sitting on a bench beside the lake
awaiting sunset far away from town,
a cool and peaceful spot. I'm here to take
some pictures while the sun is slipping down.
I wait and watch an otter in his bath;
a great blue heron pecks around in grass.
The sun begins to lower, cuts a path
across the water like a trail of glass.
The blue is paler as the colors spread;
a tinge of yellow blends to peach and pinks.
The fiery ball goes down—the sky is red.
I stand in awe, as silent as a sphinx.
The beauty of the scene has me enrapt,
My Canon sits untouched, the lens uncapped.

Category 3: Joseph A. Cavanaugh, Sr. Memorial Award

Kolette Montague
Centerville, UT

Catching Sunrise in Ireland

The trick is remembering mist
all those in-betweens—
lamb's fleece, gull's feathers
the thousand casts of silver—
fish scales, sea foam, rain soaked rocks.
And then to make some glisten—
dew, calm seas, tears.
Now find just the right grays,
a hundred of those might do.
You'll want everything from
just-this-side-of-midnight
to ocean-view blue.
Layer lightly with a watercolor brush
made of faerie hair.
Wait for a heartbeat or two,
no more than one deep breath.
Beware. It will change
in an eye blink
and never come out the same
twice in your lifetime.

Category 4: Henrietta & Mark Kroah Founders Award

Jeani M. Picklesimer
Ashland, KY

Quiver Of The Moment

brush
in hand
finds rhythm
of the master
Michelangelo
while Sistine walls
rejoice with
final strokes

Category 5: Past Presidents Award

John F. Foster
Sun City Center, FL

Glued To Food

"You are what you eat,"
nutritionists say.
So, if that's the case,
I'm a garbage can
with the lid open.

Fast food places
Don't have to ask,
"Want fries with that?"
They all know me.

Friends suggest
miracle
remedy.

I say
"Oh? I'll

Bite."

Category 6: O Hapa Days Award

Sherwood Ross
Miami, FL

The Egret

The chunky Chinese lady who lives next door
Perspiring, lugs her groceries from the store
Her lustrous black hair coiled beneath
Her "DKNY" cap
She'll eat her breakfast orange
Then ask me if I want a nap.
Having other lovers as well, she savors her intrigue
But I awoke on rag doll legs
And beg off citing my fatigue. Outside,
A white egret alights from a cloudless sky
And struts grand as any king across the street
Motorists stop to let him pass them by
Chest out, head thrusting forward
With every step on golden feet.

I wonder if egrets mate for life
Or are they restless sensualists
Indulging casual affairs.
Can I strut like a kind when I cross a street?
I put my clothes on and I descend the stairs.
The Chinese lady watches me leave
My form reflected in her black and shining eyes
I have robbed her of an opportunity for intrigue
And the thrill that comes from telling lovers' lies.
How quaint our world must appear
To egrets looking down upon our dwellings from above
Upon us mortals, male and female
Who do not mate for life yet
Wonder why we long for love.

Category 7: The Nostalgia Award

Lorraine H. Ruhl
Flagler Beach, FL

Exit, Unscripted

You've left me to tread a lonely stage,
Our well-rehearsed lines, my soliloquies.
Though we've played best friends from an early age,
You've left me to tread a lonely stage.
No dialogue on the playwright's page,
No prompting of mutual memories—
You've left me to tread a lonely stage,
Our well-rehearsed lines, my soliloquies.

Category 8: Story Time Award

Sherwood Ross
Miami, FL

O, Guitar!

O, guitar! Let my hands rejoice on your strings once more
And I will play the old ballads as we stroll
These red cobblestone streets of the inner harbor
Wet with the spume flung off the night-black sea
The sea that brings the eager sailors to our shore
The French and English, American, and Dutch
To marvel at our music, slake their thirst and
To satiate their lust.
They gather where my troubadour father,
Like his father before him,
Lingered to play at each sidewalk café, to play
Their guitars in the green gardens of Rio
Serenading sailors, tourists, and streetwalkers alike
Under the five stars of the Southern Cross.

I remember my father's guitar calling
The Carioca street-boys to follow and dance
Along Avenue Atlantica. Calling the Carioca girls
To flare their skirts and bare their legs
And shake breasts covered by thin bandanas
As they danced along the moon-silvered sands
Of Ipanema and Copacabana.

Down beckoning boulevards
My father led singers and dancers
Followed by the street urchins and tag-along tramps
Their faces flickering on and off as old movie footage
In the sputtering light of the faint street lamps.
I hear my father now
Speak-sing his words in his seductive bass
Playing the love songs of Villa-Lobos and Jobim
Radiant from the inner joy illuminating his face.

Now let us climb to the crest of Sugar Loaf
To play at the foot of Christ the Redeemer
Who alone understands our hurt and pain.
Jesus, I will play the song of the bees for you
As I have never played it before!
I will pour their intoxicating honey into your ears
Our Sambas will rise to your outstretched arms
Music to move even a Christ sculpted from stone.
Our notes will dance on your fingertips and arms
Arms that welcome all the world to our Brazilian home.

Look up! From star-rise to star-set
We have played another night away
So that of all the stars Venus alone lingers over Rio
For she does not want to quit this night of love.
Yet a fireball sun is rising over the ocean
With its promise of a new day of music
Beginning each morning with my mother
Opening the kitchen window of our cottage
Singing to the Blue Petral
Singing to the White-winged Swallow
Who flutter in familiarly to share our daily bread
And to hear Mother's pure soprano
Each note quavering with sunlit joy
That begins my day as I rise from bed.

O, guitar! My love and consolation
May your rhythms ever beat in time with the rhythm of my heart
Hold me forever in your thrall. When death comes
Yours is the voice I shall miss most of all. O, guitar!

Category 9: A Poet's Vision

John McBride
Bettendorf, IA

Fishing Wonder Lake

What they fish for changes
as light changes on water.
It's more than whitefish, pickerel, salmon.

There's a space in their mind
where they die. They brick it up,
they bricked it up a long time ago.

Their lines are invisible, but not their lures.
They love them the way misers,
even when they must talk, count ceaselessly.

They love them feathered, or striped,
or making a silver curve that flashes in sunlight
at the slightest flick of the wrist.

If they could send their eyes out on a hook
and return them to their sockets, they would,
if they could use their hearts for bait, they might.

There's something they have never caught,
something that makes them stand there every day,
waiting, casting, reeling in.

It's different each time. The water's
different, the sky, the way a seagull
hangs in the fresh morning air, or doesn't.

What they will catch grows to fill in
a lake they've never seen before,
no road out or in.

Category 10: Randall Cadman Memorial Award

Joyce Shiver
Crystal River, FL

Return To Willow Street

The houses lean together, seem to touch,
old cronies talking over olden days.
But fifty years and more ago a clutch
of roses bloomed beside one parch, a blaze
of crimson every summer. Even more,
the neighbors' lilacs purpled all our springs.
The yards were neat; the houses always wore
the look of happiness contentment brings.
It makes me sad to see the weeds and thorns,
the broken shutters, missing windows, cracked
and fallen bricks. It looks as though each mourns
for all the tender care and love they've lacked.
   I turn to leave and breathe a sad good-bye
   to old remembered friends who soon will die.

Category 11: LaVaughn Hess Memorial Award

Abbie Minard
Valencia, PA

rain landing
very softly
applauds itself

Category 12: The Ballad Award

John F. Foster
Sun City Center, FL

Echo

Slowstepping sure to dirge of drum,
their reeds a grieving moan,
proud clansman march to richest hum
of bass and treble drone.

With every swell of ruddy cheek,
bereavement bleats a tone
of woeful news, of anguish bleak:
they've lost one of their own.

The Highlands' heathered hills resound
in haunting harmony
'mid mourners aching to the sound—
a daunting elegy.

In regimental file they march,
their chanters at full tilt,
parading 'neath the graveyard's arch
in splendid vest and kilt.

To slowest beat the column plays
in reverential pride ...
The band now turns its solemn gaze
to countryman's graveside.

Sky-soaring hymn, majestic knell
salutes one of the clan.
It echoes still in distant dell,
their tribute to this man.

Category 13: Adrienne Rich Memorial Award

Janet Watson
Wesley Chapel, FL

Keepers

We traveled far, from different countries,
To discover the common culture of one.

You wake me to watch the sun rise between the pines,
But I prefer my dreams and want to return to them.

What do you think I said? This is our new game.
It never loses its novelty, is more fun than hearing aids.

Others shed loves like winter coats, not learning
Time's lesson of passion: warmth is more comfort than heat.

The years have sometimes been troubled. That hardly matters.
I cling to your voice, your thoughts, even your bad habits.

Do we argue more than we once did? Maybe the reason
Is our mortality. Grief will be less when the other is gone.

Category 14: Williard B. Foster Memorial Award

Leslie C. Halpern
Oviedo, FL

Appraisal

In a competitive market
with fluctuating cycles
of supply and demand,
scrutinized, itemized, magnified—
value increased over time.
Rare, unusual, one of a kind;
preserved in a smoke-free home,
still in original package,
condition: very fine to excellent,
only slightly used, no missing parts.
All pieces remain intact
except, perhaps, my heart.

Category 15: Seamus Heaney Memorial Award

John F. Foster
Sun City Center, FL

Without The Birds
— *A gloss poem*

We ran as if to meet the moon
That slowly danced behind the trees.
The barren boughs without the leaves,
Without the birds, without the breeze.

"Going For Water" —Robert Frost

We ran as if to meet the moon
And gaily tossed our clothes aside
To skinny dip on evening tide
And ripple water's silver brow.
It pleases me to think just how
We ran: as if to meet the moon

That slowly danced behind the trees
And winked *complicitly,* its light
For us to frolic in the night.
Upon the shore as if in dreams,
We dipped and tripped on moonlit beams
That slowly danced behind the trees.

The barren boughs without the leaves
Allowed a glimpse of owl and hawk
Who, startled, fled our playful talk.
As Nature came into our view,
We stared in wide-eyed wonder through
The barren boughs without the leaves.

Without the birds, without the breeze,
Our special place beside the sea
Would never beckon you and me.
How could a leafless landscape thrive
Or spirit and belief survive
Without the birds, without the breeze?

Category 16: The Peace Award

Mary Jo Balistreri
Genesee Depot, WI

Boating On The Yerres

Men lift the sky
    in a shower of veiled hues, wooden paddles
dipping deep in the liquid silk of the Yerres.

    With rippled strokes, they guide their skiffs,
slip silently between rows of poplars.
    A woman watches from the sanatorium, sees
trees shimmy in the skimmed wakes.

The green sheen of reeds begins to sweep her mind
    clean of all but the light, the men and the charmeuse
skein of river becoming shadows in the sun-drunk air.

Closing her eyes, she drinks the breeze, the stillness
    of this country afternoon, the lap of water on hull
As soothing as a lullaby.
    Shifts of color, luminosity flicker behind her eyelids.

In the cradle of her boat, she is alive to each vibration,
    braided into the melody of river music.

Category 17: The Live Poets Award

Brenda Miller
Orrville, OH

Or Maybe Seek The Light

The dark side of the moon we do not see,
its barren bleakness destitute and cold,
it turns away from us continually
its secrets it would better leave untold.

Its barren bleakness destitute and cold,
this black forbidding place where nothing lives;
its secrets it would better leave untold,
its wilderness the time never forgives.

This black, forbidding place where nothing lives:
deep in the so uncertain human soul. I find
its wilderness the time never forgives.
Its chains do stretch and sinuously bind

deep in the so uncertain human soul. I find
those entering there: Encounter something more.
Its chains do stretch and sinuously bind
those seeking the dark who enter through this door.

Those entering there: Encounter something ... more.
a tomb of sorts where no one feels at home.
Those seeking the dark who enter through this door,
despite what company they keep here in this gloam.

(a tomb of sorts where no one feels at home)
they are betrayed by self first, unseen alone.
Despite what company they keep. Here in this gloam
who keep them trapped—in spirit, soul, and bone—

they are betrayed by self first—unseen. Alone:
the predators roam about disguised as friends
who keep them trapped in spirit, soul, and bone.
Tied to witless ends, pretentions; the lie pretends.

The predators roam about, disguised as friends.
The greatest is the eye found in the mirror.
Tied to witless ends. Pretentions. The lie pretends
seeking the dark is what you may not fear.

The greatest is the eye. Found in the mirror,
when seeking finds the dark. That lives within—
seeking the dark. Is what you may not fear
the loss of life and time decayed by sin?

When seeking finds the dark, that lives—within.
It turns away from us. Continually.
The loss of life and time decayed by sin:
The dark side of the moon we do not see.

Category 18: June Owens Memorial Award

Betty Prisendorf
Merritt Island, FL

Rain On The River

"When the parting suddenly flings wide forever, I'll
Remember everything by your name, by the quiver
Of your wise and bashful smile." — Yocheved Bat Miriam

   All day it comes,
this wonder of steamy July,
cooling sheets of calm,
tender on the just-tossed earth,
Soft as the cat sleeping at my feet.
Roseate Spoonbills wing by.
Manatees cavort.
The mist, sudden, shifts apart,
sends Lavender beams, shimmering
like the lights in her blue-black hair.
How she loved it all.
The cat rolls and shifts—stretches serenely.
My soul struggles to follow—move away from
the flash of crushed metal, shocks of blood and
bone. I am a new strange land.
I am the Dalai Lama on the tear-stained
Road from Tibet walking a rocky path,
seeking peace.

Category 19: Miami Poets Award – Beaches

Mary Jo Balistreri
Genesee Depot, WI

Moving Meditation With High Tide In Naples

When I concede to the gulf and accept
the small space left to walk, I take off my shoes
and go barefoot. The surf rolls over my feet
like a playful retriever, rushes at my legs and licks
me with salty affection. I splash along, skirt clumps
of seaweed, briny red smell mixed with coconut
oil and a rainbow of umbrellas.

I walk. I dream in shapes of sand and air
like the children making castles. Imagination climbs
a bluebell sky, a parasail drifts among clouds,
a pelican rides the warm thermals.

Close to shore, dolphins rise and dive. Walkers point
and dreamers stop building. Those in the surf stand still.
In the perfect grace of curved bodies, in the radiance
of a sunlit sea, their leaps are revelation.

Rounding the bend at Clam pass, a great white egret
perches, huge in the tree, and opposite him, a heron.
Those ancient croaky voices seem to thank me for coming,
proper preachers after a good sermon. I turn around
to go back the way I came, an ending, a beginning.

Category 20: Tomoka Poets Award

Ellaraine Lockie
Sunnyvale, CA

First Love

The dandelion necklace
Skippy Fisher's mother made
to give me as an apology
after I hit him with a toy rifle
She—just sure
that he did something
to deserve it

Category 21: The Unforgotten Award

Janet Watson
Wesley Chapel, FL

The Predator

The crows were magistrates
in feathered robes. They blackened
the branches beyond my window,
new shadows always arriving,
shuffling into place,
their onyx eyes alert,
their throats indicting me.
Nature had sent them
to be my accusers.
I was a monster, an aberration
of all that was natural.
Poe's torment was a single raven.
My judges numbered hundreds,
all screaming the sentence of guilt—
We know, we know, we know.
I had concealed my connection
to the crimes I committed
against young and tender victims,
but the omniscient crows
would not be silenced,
and I relinquished my defense
to their raucous voices.
My death was recorded as suicide,
but, no, it was an execution
by these very birds who are now
the only visitors to my grave.
They swagger like Druids,
privy to all the terrible secrets
that live in this place of the dead.

Category 22: Winkdebleck's Challenge

Lee Pelham Cotton
Locust Hill, VA

Queen Of The Desert, Queen Of The Night

The curtain rises: sunset splashes scene
with crimson. Diva stands revealed. She waits
here, poised and plump, transmuted into queen
of lunar-stellar majesty. Her fate
ordains she reigns this night alone, then die.
Across the desert sands that blazed at noon,
nocturnal breezes serenade the sky,
enticing forth each icy star. The moon
discerns coyote ululation; cued,
illumines chaparral's far-reaching rings.
The mood is set: expectant attitude
prevails. Embracing evening, she sings
    her scented song for hours, so gold and white,
    then fades to gray in morning's mundane light.

Category 23: Gingerbread Poets Award

Trina Lee
Oklahoma City, OK

Waiting

Dreams of yesterday's kisses,
the secret, hidden times,
together in the darkness.
Now in the sunset moments
when the sky is quiet,
I reminisce.

I reminisce
about the tenderness of our first kiss
leading to passion that broke the quiet,
knowing it was stolen time,
a perfect world at the moment
protected by the darkness.

The day chases away the darkness
and I reminisce
about those precious moments,
wanting just one more kiss.
What happened to our happy times?
I feel so alone. It is so quiet.

My longing won't be quiet.
There's danger in the darkness.
It's been such a long time.
I reminisce,
remembering the warmth of your kiss,
worrying, wanting other moments.

I know there will never be a moment
when the world is safe and quiet
until I'm back in your arms, with a kiss
to chase away the darkness.
So, I reminisce,
try to pass this wistful, lonely time,

And it's been such a long time.
I'm waiting for the moment
I won't have to reminisce,
just wait in the quiet,
not fearing the darkness.
I can almost feel your kiss.

I think about our secret times, the tender kisses
turning to passion filled moments; watch day turn
to darkness and reminisce in the evening's quiet.

Category 24: Jane Opal Memorial Award

Betty Prisendorf
Merritt Island, FL

Getting Down With Old Satchmo
On Bourbon Street in New Orleans

Could even an angel play the trumpet like that?
Mack the Knife, Hello Dolly, Blueberry Hill
Rippling rises, riffs, rumbles, often a scat
Could even an angel play the trumpet like that?
White hanky mopping, our Louie's the cat!
Margaritas, two encores, this night's a thrill
Could even an angel play the trumpet like that?
Mack the Knife, Hello Dolly, Blueberry Hill.

FSPA 2014
Student Contests
Place Winners and
Honorable Mention Winners

Daytona by Niki Byram

Junior Division

First Place
Luke Favata

Norman S. Edelcup Sunny Isles Beach K-8, Dade County
Teacher: Ms. Patti Ward

Fishing on the lake,
A big one bites the bait hook.
A good catch today!

Second Place
Lisett Castellanos

Rockway Middle School, Dade County
Teacher: Kristin Trompeter

Contrasting colors
The brightness after darkness
Across the blue sky

Third Place
Grace Schultz

Fort Clarke Middle School, Alachua County
Teacher: Lauren Hiner

The Light at the End of the Tunnel

Sitting alone in a dark icy hall
You clamber slowly, with fear, to your feet.
Making your way, you will stumble and fall
Feel the gray thunder, your heart as it beats.

The path that you take is no easy way,
The long journey is treacherously rough.
Long have your eyes ached for the light of day
A child's feet have been worn weary and tough.

When the blackness stretches before your eyes
And constant footfalls seem to have no end
The tunnel will slowly begin to rise
And a warrior will turn 'round the bend.

The trials are through, your grievances passed,
An innocence grown, in the light at last.

First Honorable Mention
Andrea Garcia

Norman S. Edelcup Sunny Isles Beach K-8, Dade County
Teacher: Ms. Patti Ward

The Flower

I see the flower
Sitting on the grass
As the days pass
The flower grows bigger and brighter

Every day, I pass through the fields
I see that one flower
That stands alone
With great meaning

I think of it as a symbol
A symbol of great power
To the other flowers, it has no purpose

But to me, it means endurance
With its pink and gold colors
It is part of Mother Nature's beauty

It is, the flower

Second Honorable Mention
Dehna Rezaei

Howard Bishop Middle School, Alachua County
Teacher: Kathy Brugger

Moon

You follow me in the darkness.
You creep behind the trees.
You know all my secrets,
as I keep them with me.

For some days you disappear,
and it's always so still
but you are always here right by me,
right by that window sill.

You bring your friends,
on dark clear nights,
sparkling and dancing
across the dark sky.

Third Honorable Mention
Brett Geunes

Howard Bishop Middle School, Alachua County
Teacher: Kathy Brugger

My Golden Guitar
Fingers on strings make music
Vibrations through air

Fourth Honorable Mention
Cassidy Eliza Thimmer

Sebastian River Middle School, Indian River County
Teacher: Janet Inghram

Entrapped Within A Winter Wall Of My Own Creation

I was once encased
Covered in ice, of snow and crystal
My lips were laced
I was once encased
In a solitary prison
Drowned by the dark
With all my worries nearly risen
I was once completely bound
With no hope of being found
I was never saved from my fears
Never pulled from the depths
Of my endless ocean of tears
Until the very end
I never cease to recall
The time I was caged and couldn't speak
The time words' cold sting
Made me ever tied to the frosty keep
I was once frozen solid in a silent capture
One that bound me to my fate
And I knew not
Of whom held the key
Until that destined day
When the one with the key
Turned out to be me

Fifth Honorable Mention
Sebastian Smith

Norman S. Edelcup Sunny Isles Beach K-8, Dade County
Teacher: Patti Ward

Do They Exist?

Now I think, as I lay
All my thoughts, so unclear the color gray

The planet earth, the place I call home
But the question asked, are we alone?

We are humans, a special kind
But are there others up in space that we may find?

Infinity times infinity, the universe is so unknown
Remember E.T., E.T. phone home?

Can we talk to or see another kind
I really believe, one day we will find

Find what, you ask? What is it that I wish to see?
Aliens ...
could there really be?

Senior Division

First Place
Claire Zuo

Miami Palmetto Senior High School, Dade County
Teacher: Debra Salas

Ephemera

when I was younger,

every letter of every word
of every page of every book

was a pomegranate seed waiting
to be bitten into

heroes and heroines emerging
from paper creases

and fantasy realms materializing out
of a few serif sentences

once I walked across a traffic-laden street,
fully absorbed in Judy Blume

I held books beneath desks
while my fourth-grade teacher lectured

on the ins and outs of long division

I mutinied against my parents
by reading under flashlight past my bedtime

but my lexicon's inflation compensated
for the thick glasses I was forced to wear

but now books appear almost like phantoms
eidolons of nostalgia for times when

my time wasn't pervaded
by a relentless inundation

of GPAs and Extracurriculars
and Club Officer Positions

I long not for innocence or
to relive some romanticized childhood

but only to be able to again read

with the same freedom and fervor as I once did,
and to see words behind my closed eyelids

Second Place
Taylor Ramirez

Hillsborough Virtual School, Hillsborough County
Teacher: N/A

Freak Show

Welcome to the circus; what is your expertise?
Will you walk the tightrope or ask for the trapeze?
Will you place your head inside of the lion's massive mouth?
Or will you slip into a clown car then struggle to get out?

We can look into the future! Come on, just take a glance.
Pick a card, any card; it's all a game of chance.
Grab an old Ouija board. We'll play a round or two.
But careful what you ask about— it might come after you.

Look at all the girls wearing skin-tight Hollister shirts,
And the guys are watching for the ones with the shortest skirts.
Don't you feel imperfect next to plastic and unreal?
Let's put them into a cage and show them how we feel ...

This is the freak show! Where nothing goes as planned.
No matter how well we explain, society can't understand.
They are cruel and they are vile. Let's lock them up
Before they go wild.
They'll be the main attraction!
Oh, won't this just be grand!

I tell the world, "Ladies and Gentlemen,
Boys and Girls,
Behind this curtain are creatures—
strangest there's ever been.
They only follow with the crowd or refuse to be seen.
They laugh at us because of how we act and dress
They think we are wrong for standing out from the rest."

Isn't it confusing how we are told to be unique,
and we get shot down and forced to hold
our heads in defeat?
No matter what they tell us, we are not the sin!
We will rise against them all! Together we are sure to win!

Third Place
Jacob Herman

New World School of the Arts, Dade County
Teacher: Christian Losa

All Hallow's Eve

When children's shadows lengthen fast and fade,
When dark facades let masks be more obscure,
When midnight moonlight makes a nightly shade,
Here dance the hallowed creatures we procure.

The wicked one who cackles through her fire,
The cold one with his skin an iv'ry pale,
The cursed one who emerges from the briar,
The torn one seldom seen beyond the veil.

They gather underneath the glowing light,
And praise their Pagan gods with chants of thanks.
They venture through the dusk to make their plight,
And designate the drunkards to their ranks.

So watch for shadows, hidden and discreet,
For they may grant you much more trick than treat.

First Honorable Mention
Caitlin McBride

Mariner High School, Lee County
Teacher: Jennifer Christiansen

Bangladesh Rain

The rain flows sideways.
There is no use of an umbrella.
In the pouring rain, she rows her boat
As if it was a shark parting the waves.
She paddles away from the savage ruckus.
The world becomes silent in Bangladesh.
She sees many people, but hears nothing.
The city stares her in the face.
She becomes blinded by thick droplets.
And her world becomes fuzzy.
Water quickly fills her boat.
There is no place to run.
She is stranded.
She is trapped.
The rain flows sideways.

Second Honorable Mention
Aubrey Osiborski

Spruce Creek High School, Volusia County
Teacher: Todd Palmer

Ode to the Cross

I remember that almost-forgotten present
You hid under the tree for me to find.
Inside was a tiny silver cross
That I hadn't come to cherish yet.

How you worried
That winged cross would end up hanging
Alone and forgotten
And it did

Until the sixth hour
When darkness fell on that hospital room.
And on the ninth hour
You fell back into cardiac arrest
Followed by the stroke that ended it all.
Then you yielded your final breath
And with it, your spirit.

After you left this world too soon
I searched endlessly
For anything to remember you by
And found that tiny silver cross
You left behind.

Every day that's gone by

Since that April sixteenth
Your final gift to me
Has rested on my heart.
Because that was the day
You were freed from your cross
And I was nailed to mine.

Third Honorable Mention
Sierra Blair

Dreyfoos School of the Arts, Palm Beach County
Teacher: Brittany Rigdon

The Last Dragon

The last of the dragons and she's nothing but human
Liquid fire for blood and wings too big for her clumsy body
Magic spills into words from her fingertips but nobody listens
She locks herself away inside the caverns
Of her mind and guards her treasures, abandoned
She is a secret that must be hidden
Or she would break so many hearts
And none more than yours
But who would think of her heart
Already broken, beating and bleeding between her claws
She does it all for you, not that you would notice
Not that you would care
The bond between you she nurtures like an egg
Praying that when the time comes
She won't be forced to let go
Shredded letters she never sent and
Words you probably never read
She would breathe the fire of life into you
When you couldn't go on any longer
And still she would be in the background

Of your thoughts, supporting, fiercely protecting
Just a shadow, here and then gone in an instant
Never thanked, never lifted up, never acknowledged
And she doesn't ask for anything, she never has,
Too afraid of greed and selfishness
She just wants you to smile,
So she'll live high above the world
All alone in her cave where she can't hurt anyone
Guarding her treasures and waging war against demons
And that's where she'll die
And then there will be no more dragons

Only dust

Fourth Honorable Mention
Diane Petit-Frere

William H. Turner Technical Arts High School, Dade County
Teacher: Tangela Allen

Her Arms Cry Help

She was marked
Marked by the cruel words and insecurities
etched in her skin
Labeling her as inferior, making her nothing
but an outcast, a loser
Marked by the criss-crossing scars decorating her arms
Branding her a slave to the evils of humanity
Reminding her why she will never be good enough,
but just an outcast, a loser
This girl walks down the halls with her head bowed
in defeat and her face a stone wall—
Like Jericho, she wills herself not to crumble
from the enemy's shouts all around
Yet the teasing and taunting grows louder,
making her wish she was deaf—or dead
Their watching eyes like daggers pierce into her skin,
burning it under their judging gaze
Wishing her flaws were invisible,
she prays to her tears not to surrender
Cornered by her attackers,
she finds refuge in an empty room
as she shelters her spirit from them
A cry for help dies on her lips and
rises again on her arms, haunting her
So she breaks through the barrier of flesh and
releases it along with her frustrations
And then hides behind a cover-up
of long sleeves and dark hoodies

Queued up wounds mimic her life line;
short and painful
They start to heal until cut again
by a wicked tongue or sharp razor
Superficial cuts trace the cracks in her heart
and blood drips as her body weeps pain
Once again she finds herself at death's door
but like always she is rejected
She is not even good enough to die;
she cannot bleed out her imperfections—but she can try
An artist with a razor, her arms are her canvas
as she draws out her pleading cry
But her work remains anonymous,
her masterpiece unknown
Nothing but a series of accidents and fabricated lies
But her arms tell a story—they are a tragedy;
Evidence in the crime scene of an unsolvable case
But can they crack it before it cracks her?
For she is running out of space
There's only so much her poor arms can take—
she needs to be saved before it's too late
Crucified by her peers, she must pay the uncommitted sins
for which she is guilty
So she suffers in silence, resigned to be the subject
of the whispers and rumors
But buried deep, the cry for help in there;
her eyes, sad and lifeless, ask for it
Her soul, broken and battered beg for it;
and if you listen closely, her arms cry help, too

Fifth Honorable Mention
Garrett Johnson

Spruce Creek High School, Volusia County
Teacher: Todd Palmer

Cry, Beloved Kenya
—Based on true events and
Cry the Beloved Country

When your homeland is ripped apart by those
Who would kill you—
Your friends,
Your family,
But you are on the other side of the world,
What do you do?

When you see children
Pulled by screaming parents
In terror of impending death
Running for cover from gunfire
What do you do?

When you hear the gunshots
The petrified babies screaming
And the wounded shrieking
In your mind's eye
And can't shut them out
What do you do?

The murderers stand where you once stood
Desecrating your place of home
Hunting humans for their disbelief
Executioners turban-clad,
Guns at their side.
What do you do?

You cry.
You weep.
For the pain suffered
For the tears shed
For the blood poured out
On the forsaken ground.
You sing the song the broken sing,
For the women and children are away
And they can sing no more.

FSPA OFFICERS and CHAPTERS

CURRENT FSPA OFFICERS

Joseph (Joe) Cavanaugh, *President*
Walter (Teal) Mims, *Vice President*
Mary-Ann Westbrook, *Secretary*
Judith Krum, *Treasurer*

CURRENT CERTIFIED FSPA CHAPTERS

Big Bend Poets, Tallahassee
Gingerbread Poets, Crystal River
Live Poets Society, Daytona Beach
Miami Poets, Pinecrest (Miami-Dade)
New River Poets, Pasco County
Orlando Area Poets, Maitland
Poetry for the Love of It, Tallahassee
Poetry Ocala, Ocala
Space Coast Poetry Club, Merritt Island
Sunshine Poets, Crystal River
Third Dimension Poets, Broward County
Tomoka Poets, Ormond Beach

FSPA also has many members at large who are not affiliated with a chapter. These members live not only in Florida, but in various states across the country and countries around the globe. New members and chapters are always welcome to join FSPA. Rules and requirements are on the FSPA website: www.floridastatepoetsassocition.org.

FLORIDA STATE POETS ASSOCIATION

The Florida State Poets Association, Inc. was founded in 1974 by Henrietta A. Kroah of DeLand, Florida, with the assistance of Han Jurgenson, PhD, of the University of Tampa, a past president of the National Federation of State Poetry Societies (NFSPS). Its main objective is to secure a fuller public recognition of the art of poetry, stimulate a finer and more intelligent appreciation of poetry, and to provide opportunities for the study of poetry and incentives for the writing and reading of poetry. A State Convention is held each October and a springtime conference is in April.

Visit: www.**floridastatepoetsassociation.org** for current events, activities, and member news

NATIONAL FEDERATION OF STATE POETRY SOCIETIES

NFSPS is a federation of over thirty state poetry societies. Organized in 1959 and incorporated in 1966, NFSPS provides support to the state member societies through a quarterly newsletter, various national contests, and a convention each June. Over the years FSPA members have been an integral part of the federation. The 2015 NFSPS convention will be held in St. Petersburg, Florida.

Visit: www.**nfsps.com** for further information

CPSIA information can be obtained at www.ICGtesting.com
Printed in the USA
LVOW05s1056141014

408681LV00002B/3/P